Marie Herbert

The Bible; its Influence, its Relations to Republican Government

And its Necessity as a Text-Book of Ethics in the Public Schools

Marie Herbert

The Bible; its Influence, its Relations to Republican Government
And its Necessity as a Text-Book of Ethics in the Public Schools

ISBN/EAN: 9783337096137

Printed in Europe, USA, Canada, Australia, Japan

Cover: Foto ©Lupo / pixelio.de

More available books at **www.hansebooks.com**

THE BIBLE;

Its Influence; its Relations to Republican Government, and its Necessity as a Text-Book of Ethics in the Public Schools.

By MARIE HERBERT.

"England made Shakspeare, and the Bible made England."—*Victor Hugo.*
"The first principles of our government are the truths of Divine Revelation."—*Webster.*

SAN FRANCISCO:
Cubery & Company, Publishers, 414 Market Street, below Sansome.
1876.

PREFACE.

BELIEVING that the Bible is a revelation from God, given both for spiritual enlightenment and as a great popular text-book, from which may be drawn a clear knowledge of those ethical principles upon which human society can alone successfully build individual and public character, I have in my spare moments prepared this little volume, which, it is hoped, will be found to contain at least a few grains of truth, and be instrumental in awaking with some a more correct comprehension of the essentiality of the Sacred Scriptures in the developing of a healthy social and civil life.

Political and social reformers are constantly and ostentatiously laboring to correct public abuses, and to impel the race forward toward the ideal; but it is only where the Bible becomes the source of popular inspiration that we find an active reformatory spirit and a permanent progressive movement. And it is this great fact, which I wish to indelibly impress upon the minds of my countrymen, that they may be enabled to discharge with fidelity and with honor those sacred trusts of conscience and of liberty which a beneficent Providence has committed to their care.

The writer is not unconscious of the penalties as well as rewards of authorship. Silence may bring disappointment, and criticism may bring agony of spirit. But having supreme faith in the indestructibility and omnipotence of truth, we scatter the golden kernels in the manner most in consonance with the inspirations of our soul, trusting in the fructifying influences of the gentle dews and wooing sunshine, which ever, in the fullness of the season, bring forth the sheaf, and then the bread.

SAN FRANCISCO, Sept. 11, 1875.

THE BIBLE;

Its Influence; its Relations to Republican Government, and its Necessity as a Text-Book of Ethics in the Public Schools.

"Tell me where the Bible is, and where it is not, and I will write a moral geography of the world."

Was significantly remarked by a certain tourist whose observations were not alone confined to art-galleries, museums, old architecture, classic ruin, and historic reminiscence—material expression of buried generations—but were more especially directed to the spiritual manifestations of the present—the character, homes and institutions of the living. The proposition, though embodying an idea popularly recognized as a relic of Puritanism—too antique and dogmatic for this self-sufficient, speculative, and commercial age, is nevertheless fundamental in character, vital in relationship, and broad in its reachings as are the necessities of the common weal; involving as it does, political and social, as well as moral conditions.

Unworthy of consideration though it may be deemed by the sensuous masses, it possesses, notwithstanding, for the statesman equally with the ethologist, a

Skepticism may weave its subtle theories: Materialism may shed, as the diviner revelation, its pale light upon the human understanding; and still, the written Word of God stands, and will stand forever, as the chief primate in the true development of man. Therefore, as suggested in the proposition we quote, the Bible is the grand criterion of morality, of social and civil progress, and of the latent resource of nations. So effective, so uniform, so distinctive is it in its influences in developing character, that we need only inquire by what firesides it is cherished, and from what hearth-stones it is rejected, to be able not only to determine the moral character of communities, but to point out upon the world's map the great centres of popular intelligence, of useful industry, of individual dignity, of physical health and comfort, of personal grace and beauty, as well as to draw prophetic outlines of the civil and social destiny of peoples.

The logic of all authentic modern history unequivocally confirms what is here assumed wringing even from the skeptic Gibbon the declaration, that wherever the Sacred Scriptures form the basis of religious faith, there do we find " the most distinguished portion of human kind in arts and learning as well as in arms;" and from Hume, the apologist of royalty and its vices; the traducer of republican virtues and of the Christian faith, the admission that the great spring of popular action under the English Commonwealth "—the period when, he admits, England retrieved her lost power upon the Continent, and established it upon the sea, " was the inspiration of revealed religion."— The " fanaticism," as he terms it of the Puritans, that class whose moral and intellectual forces were drawn from their Bibles and their hymn-books.

The testimony of an observing American who visited Europe a few years prior to the subversion of the Papal States is not inapplicable here. He says: "One glance of the eye will inform you where the Bible is and where it is not. Go to Italy: decay, destruction, suffering, meet you on every side. Commerce droops, agriculture sickens, the useful arts languish. There is a heaviness in the air. You feel cramped by some invisible power. The people dare not speak aloud; they walk slowly; an armed soldiery is around their dwellings; the armed police take from the stranger his Bible before he enters the territory.

"Ask for the Bible in the book-store, it is not there; if so, in a form so expensive as to be beyond the reach of the common people. The preacher takes no text from the Bible. Enter the Vatican and inquire for the Bible, and you will be pointed to some case where it reposes among prohibited books, side by side with the works of Diderot, Rousseau, and Voltaire. But pass over the Alps into Switzerland, and down the Rhine into Holland, and over the Channel to England and Scotland, and what an amazing contrast meets the eye? Men and women look with an air of independence. There are industry, neatness, thrift, instruction for children. Why this difference? There are no brighter skies — there are no fairer scenes;" but, he says, "they have the Bible."

And it is here, in the light of divine Revelation, that humanity has written, and is still writing, its grandest epics. It is here that the loftiest ideals of the pure and the just, the heroic and sublime, are most nearly approached. God's written law is no less certain in its ultimate effects upon mind receptive than is His unwritten law in its effects upon matter.

Under its influence the soul develops into forms of beauty and of strength, prototypes of which are only found in the purely spiritual and purely divine, reaching back even into the mind of the Infinite.

Its influence, inherently sovereign, must finally be accepted by the social and political reform as the only means of radical and permanent improvement; as the only moral analeptic in which diseased and retrogressive communities can have reasonable hope.

Mazzarin sought to soften and refine the manners of France through the opera and the ballet. Lossing dreamed of reforming the world through the power of the drama. Kant seized upon ideas and upon pure reason as the forces by which he could perfect a sublime morality and establish the universal republic. Cervantes, Robinson, Goldsmith, Dickens, Hawthorne, George Elliot, Mrs. Southworth, Arthur, and others, have thought to ennoble humanity through the novel and the romance. The Goughs would reform depraved appetites and elevate the social standard through prohibitory statutes and the persuasive power of the rostrum. The Stantons would correct social abuses and sublimate the race, until, "like the Beatrice of Dante it waits upon divine inspiration," through the force of permissive laws and the ballot for woman; but all these agents, adopted, have failed in their mission to the soul, and will fail, because, lacking the divinity that awakens the fundamental forces of moral being, no conscience kindles or responds to their calls.

So distinguished a scientist as Baron Liebig has said, that the civilization of a people may be best measured by the quantity of soap consumed; and that another has discovered that the commercial demand for iron is the best criterion of moral and social advancement; and that still another finds, like Mazzarin, that the songs of a nation form the best index of its progress and refinement. But, while it is true that soap and ballads do indicate, to a large degree, taste and sentiment, and iron invention and industry, it will be ascertained, by observation and statistics, that the most refined civilization is best measured by the number of Bibles found at the firesides and the altars of a people. And we shall also find that even the consumption of soap and the demand for iron increase, as well as the merit of ballads improve, in exact ratio with the popular desire for Bibles.

There exists no longer doubt that that people whose models of moral excellence are most faithfully drawn from the inspired Word are able to present the most refined manners, the largest industries, the noblest charities, the purest literature, the most varied arts, the most equitable laws, the most stable government, and even the most invincible armies. True, there have been peoples with philosophies, laws, literature, industries, and military renown, without the Bible; but the civilization of the most distinguished of these was no more than a brilliant prolepsis of that which was to come; no more than genius, in the dawn of its inspiration, struggling for immortal embodiment in the graces of the material, in the subtleties of dialectics, in the eloquence of harangues, in the speculations of philosophy, and in the achievement of arms. Those inspiring glimpses of the attributes of the Godhead, those lofty ideals of the pure in morals, those enrapturing visions of a future life, those grand and mighty impulses of enlightened thought, those broad utilities and charities which so mark the reign of Christian law, have no place in the civilization or philosophy of such.

Greece has left an enduring impress upon the world. Her temples, her sculpture, her poetry, her oratory, her philosophy, and her arms have given her an immortal memory. And yet, while these were giving her immortality, she was not only trampling upon the manhood of more than half her people, but her manners were course, her social tastes impure, her charities mean, her industries narrow, her ambitions barbarous, and her arms, when over the ages they cross with those of the Christian, are weak and unequal.

Had Paul found upon the Athenian altar this inscription: " To the Known God — the Supreme, Eternal One, Absolute Lawgiver, Teacher, Father;" and if with this sublime Theism he could have found interwoven into the popular heart the Messianic hope that so kindled the vision of the Hebrew prophets, or that even which seemed to so tinge the faith of their own " divine Plato," he might have so planted there the new philosophy that Greece would not have expired at Corinth, but would have survived the rudest shocks of barbarism, and given us a history far more inspiring than that which we now have, in the most brilliant chapters of her marbles, her philosophy, her eloquence, her epics, or her valor.

And, too, if Paul could have found Rome without a Pantheon — Rome, monotheistic; and if at the close of the apostolic period the gospels of Christ, instead of the poems of Hesiod, could have been the source of popular inspiration, not only Greece might have escaped the fury of the Roman eagles, but Rome might have escaped the fiery vengeance of Alaric, and the present hour of civilization have struck centuries ago.

Tyndall, in his Belfast address, draws a parallel between Mohammedan and Christian civilization, at the time of the Moorish occupancy of Spain, in favor of the former. With seeming unfairness he virtually forces Draper upon this point into antagonism with Christianity. In quoting him in support of his own views, he says, "With the intrusion of the Moors into Spain, cleanliness, order, learning, and refinement took the place of their opposites. When smitten with disease, the Christian peasant resorted to a shrine; the Moorish to an instructed physician. They encouraged translations from the Greek philosophers, but not from the Greek poets. They turned with disgust from the lewdness of our classical mythology, and denounced as an unpardonable blasphemy all connection between the impure Olympian Jove and the Most High God." He further quotes as evidence of the superior activity of the Saracenic intellect and liberality of the Mohammedan faith that, "Plato, in his absurd notions of the emission of light by the eye, was first corrected by an Arabian. That it was an Arabian who first discovered atmospheric refraction; who first explained the enlargement of the sun and moon, and the shortening of their vertical diameters when near the horizen; who first constructed a table of specific gravities; improved the hydrometer; invented the method of measuring time by pendulum oscillation;" and that, in short, it was the Mohammedan, and not the Christian, who at this period was unfolding the sciences and cultivating the intellect of the age. But is it the inciting, the enlightening, the tolerant, the pure and sublime philosophy of Christ which the subtle lance of this skeptic would so skillfully pierce? or is it a mere phantom—a corruption of the real essence—an equal triad of idolatry, skepticism, and formal Christianity which we acknowledge did then hold its scepter, not only over Catholic Spain, but over Catholic Europe, and which we willingly admit was far less favorable to the advancement of the sciences, and of civilization, than were the then pure Theism and rigid precepts of Mohammed?

And is this distinguished scientist prepared to deny that the superior activity of the Arabian intellect and the greater liberality of the Islam faith toward the sciences, the arts, and literature at this period was not after all due to the influences of the Bible, upon which he well knows Mohammed reared his great structure of theology?

Will not a knowledge of the true God, of Christ, even as a prophet, of a promised Comforter, of a resurrection, of a judgment, of an immortal life, have an inspiring and elevating effect upon the soul, even though mingled with crudities and extravagant verbiage, as in the Koran?

The Pentateuch, the Psalms, and the Gospels were the foundation of the faith of Mohammed; and, through him, these it were surely that kindled, directed, and liberalized the Moorish intellect when in the mediæval centuries it came in conflict with the enslaved and debauched spirit of the nominal Christian. But if Tyndall here really means to discriminate against Christianity, let him come down from his chosen period and draw a parallel to-day between Christ and Mohammed. If the Koran then was superior to the Bible in inciting the intellect and inspiring the hearts of men, why the contrast now?

Mohammed, in fact, but little more than unified semi-barbarism; although, as an incident of the plan, he did for a time arouse the higher life of the Saracen and the Moor with borrowed inspiration. But Christ is slowly destroying the unities of Mohammed, as well as those of all false theologies and creeds; and is not as an incident, but as a grand design, awaking for all time the higher life of all peoples ; and is steadily building an empire under whose quickening and genial sway the written and unwritten philosophies of God will finally harmonize as parts of a grand and sublime unity.

It is not from the Theogony of the Greek, the Vedas of the Hindu, or the Zenda of the Persian, nor from the Koran of the Mohammedan, but from the Bible of the Christian that modern society has imbibed its purest ideas of ethics; that letters and art have drawn their loftiest expressions ; that science and industry have derived the spirit of their grandest conquests ; that charity has gathered the inspirations of its sweetest victories; that law has received the principles of its divinest equities; and that arms even have caught the light that has led to the most brilliant and enduring triumphs.

The perfect in civilization and government can spring from no other source than the Bible; for among all the systems of religion and ethics which the world has had given it, the human soul only here finds the satisfaction, the fullness of its spiritual, moral, and social needs—that the grand " Ultimate " of the intellectual and the just, the pure and the beautiful, the meek and the majestic, the merciful and the mighty, is revealed to us in an unmistakable personality—a defined and real presence.

Philosophy attempts to discover in Nature an infinite " Satisfaction " for the emotional and intellectual necessities of man; but, after following natural law through all its complex ramifications to the utmost limit of the experimental; after tracing organic life through all its innumerable series of evolutions, down through the ages and æons of ages, to even the atom and the germ, at last finds itself at the boundary of the realm of material law, still unsatisfied, confounded, overwhelmed, even as was the "Human Spirit" in the "Dream of Richter," seeking in the midst of infinite creations for outermost suns, for frontier worlds.

And it is only in the Inspired Word that we find not alone the true God—the "Grand Ultimate" of the infinite aspirations and longings of the soul—but those great fundamental social ideas, the common Fatherhood of God; the common brotherhood of man; the common heirship of life immortal—a divine triology, by which the vital problems of sociology and of government can only be satisfactorily solved.

The despotism of superior intellect and power through all time has imposed its wrongs upon the masses; and, as a result, the inherent sense of individual right from the beginning has periodically manifested itself in some form of popular discontent. The contest, however, down through all the cycles of history to nearly our own epoch, has been fruitless, simply because no "Pillar of Fire" awakened, illuminated, and etherialized the faith of the oppressed. It was only when the sublime truths of the Bible awoke the spiritual life of man; only when these thrilled the great chords of popular thought; only when armies marched to the chant of Hebrew poetry and bayonets flashed in the light of the Cross, that human bonds began to break; that germs of equal law began to crystalize; that the people began to move by divine impulse to their true places in government, and that science, art, and civilization began their final march to the conquest of the world. And it will ever be found that in exact proportion to the influences which God's Written Law has over popular thought will government become popularized, and civilization become progressive. True, free government ostensibly graces the history of some of the earlier periods, even at the time when divine revelation was yet but slowly descending upon Judea: but it is there only as a historic embellishment. Roman as well as Grecian liberty, in a correct sense, was but a splendid political mockery. It was, in fact, no more than a polyarchy of caste—an aristocracy in which popular right had no recognition. In mediæval history free government claims acknowledgment; but neither the victory of Legnano, the prosperity of Venice, nor the eloquent enthusiasm of Rienzi could establish it upon a rational and permanent basis; simply because the Bible, with its fundamental ideas of human rights and of equal law, had not yet become the common heritage of the people. Had the Church of the Middle Ages been true to her obligations—had she but been a faithful exponent of the cause she claimed to represent, Italian liberty may then have been established to the enduring benefit of all succeeding periods.

In modern times France has repeatedly attempted the establishing of free government; but failure has constantly followed, because her religious and moral faith springs from no higher source than the philosophy of her "Encyclopedists," or of the dogmas of a corrupt theology. True and substantial self-government with her is impossible, until she emancipates her faith and rises above the materialism and superstition which now fetter her aspirations for freedom.

Edmond About would have it that France is a sick soldier of God, only needing, as a remedy, the lapse of time; but he should have said France is a sick soldier of the Triumvirate—Cæsarism, Ecclesiasticism, and Atheism; needing, as a remedy, a free Bible, a free conscience, and then time.

The hopeful but unphilosophic have confidence in her present experiment to construct free government; but, like all preceding efforts, it must fail; because Christ, the Inspiration of the true Republic, has not yet supplanted Voltaire, Pompadour, and the Pope, in the popular heart. When France, in her love, gathers up from exile the ashes of her Christian reformers, and places them as tenderly in her Pantheon as she has those of her Paladins* and of her great Infidel† then, and only then, shall we see streaking the horizon the morning of her freedom.

The very first step of departure with France in the new line of government was a violation of a great fundamental moral and social law, a law founded in human necessity and indissolubly linked with human prosperity. Following in the moral track of the Empire, the Republic of 1870, in its first work of organization, as well as in subsequent elections, trampled, with all the fearlessness of Paganism, upon the Christian Sabbath; betraying thereby, in the beginning, that want of moral integrity which is vital to the successful establishing of free government. Could John Calvin have inspired the French heart with the spirit of the Reformation as did Luther that of the German,

---

* Turenne, Vauban, Napoleon.
† Voltaire.

France might now, with her aspirations, not only be able to build up a grand structure of popular sovereignty, but she might have saved herself the humiliation of her late defeats. The Bible at her firesides would, in the three centuries since Calvin, not only have made more peaceful, more grand, and more mighty her history, but would have silently built about her a bulwark, against which neither the diplomacy of Bismarck nor the artillery of William could have prevailed.

It was the great truths of the Divine Word, scattered centuries in advance by the Jeromes of Prague, the Husses and the Luthers, that laid the foundation of the triumph of the German arms at Metz, at Strasbourg, and at Sedan; and that, finally, not only revenged at Paris international wrongs of two hundred years, but great social and religious crimes which France had so long committed against the Christian world. And these same great truths are now in turn destined, in the fullness of God's time, to lead to the overthrow of German Imperialism, and to build upon its ruins a great empire of republican law.

Love of personal independence is the old and distinguishing passion of the German heart. Liberty of thought and of will, and loyalty to conscience are its historic ideals. This spirit dominated in rude and turbulent forms in the ages of Tacitus and of Lucien, and reached its grandest climax in the devastations and wrath of Alaric. "I feel a secret and preternatural impulse to march to the gates of Rome," said the barbarian chief, in reply to the Christian zealot; and Rome finally, at midnight, reeling with debauch, burned and bled at the blast of the Gothic trumpet. "We steer as the winds direct. They will transport us to the guilty coast whose people have provoked the divine justice," said Genseric to his pilot; and now licentious Rome burned and bled at the hands of the Vandal.

Germanic liberty finally subverted by feudalism, the descendants of warlike and democratic ancestors now seek its restoration through the peaceful influences of philosophy. To regain it, theorists violate the reverence of ages, trampling down faiths, dogmas, and traditions. In search for it, they subject to fiery analysis the universe of matter and of spirit, marching with audacious step and with profane criticism, under the cover of dialectics, to the very throne even of the Infinite. And still the instinctive and supreme idea — liberty — has not yet become embodied again in sensible form. Afar in the regions of theory are hovering still, in divine idea, the republics of Kant and of Fichte, waiting to descend for embodiment in written constitutions and statutes. This realization, however, will not come through the speculations of philosophy, but only through the facts of revelation. Through the theses of the great Reformer,* and not through the hypotheses of the philosopher, is germinating and steadily strengthening, down deep at the social foundations, the revolutionary force that is finally to restore to the German — refined, embodied, legalized — his ancient liberties.

It is here, in the stormy polemics and sublime dialectics of Luther, that we find the inspirations of the prophetic revolution of Hein — that revolution in whose awful conflicts lost and subverted rights are to be regained, and out of which is to rise, above the ruins of monarchism, the genius of constitutional lib-

---
* Luther.

erty. Luther, and not Spinoza, nor Kant, nor Fichte, nor Hegal, nor Schelling, nor even Leibnitz or Goethe, will become in the hour of freedom the great glory of the Germanic race.

Ireland weeps, counts her beads, and offers her blood for the restoration of her ancient honor. But her prayers are unanswered, her dreams of sovereignty pass unfulfilled; and will, until the people become their own interpreters of God's Written Law, and accept that great moral Code as the source of inspiration. If this gifted, this brave, and immortally hopeful race would be free, they must first place Bibles at their firesides and at their altars; and then free empire may have foundation in the free thought and untrameled faith of the people. Let this be the initial revolution of Ireland, and the period may come when either her hopes of freedom will be realized or her bond of union with Anglo-Saxon destiny will become congenial or more closely knit.

Tyndall would preserve Ireland from "spiritual and intellectual tyranny," and, as a corollary, from political, by "flashing upon the minds of her youth the mild light of science;" but spiritual and intellectual chains are already upon her Catholic masses, and it is not in the "flashings of the mild light of science," nor in the dull gloamings of pantheistic materialism, as all history affirms, but in the effulgence, the fiery essence of the Divine Word, that these chains will melt.

England, with her Bibles, will always make laws for Ireland, with her dogmas. And England with her Bibles will yet become too strong for England with her kings. God's Law, with broken seal, in the English homes, chapels, and libraries, is slowly but irresistably lifting the masses in the political as well as social scale, and educating them for the exercise of sovereign prerogatives.

Had Austria welcomed Luther and the Reformation, as did Saxony, Brunswick, and Prussia, her battalions 300 years after would not have been scattered at Sadowa and her national prestige lost. Her new faith would have removed the weakness which centuries of superstition and ecclesiastical tyranny had brought; and then no field of disaster would have entombed her pride, and no hopeless oaths would have been written in blood to revenge the triumphs of the Prussian needle-gun.

Russia, that colossus of empire and of Cæsarism, with its chaos of tongues, of barbarisms, of civilizations, of sects, of sentiments, and of ideas, is beginning to quicken and thrill in all its living atoms under the inspirations of the Divine Word. As matter in its primitive, chaotic state, moves in lines of order and aggregates into the beautiful crystal, and finally into the luminous world, under the subtle laws of attraction, affinity and crystalization, so are the confused and social elements of this great empire of violence and of antagonisms, under the silent and mysterious influences of the Revealed Word, slowly but surely and grandly crystalizing into a harmonious creation of Sclavonic individuality and power. Through the colporteur and the Holy Synod of the Greek Church the Bible is being freely circulated throughout the imperial domain; and, as a result, is gradually creating an improved spiritual and social life—a new and mighty moral force, not only in the cottages of the tradesman and the artisan, but in the palaces of the nobles, in the dwellings of 20,000,000 of manumitted serfs, in the cabin of the exile, and in the tent even of the nomad Tartar—a moral force which is destined to work out that great problem of ideal freedom which so inspired the genius and burdened the prophetic spirits of Hertzen, of Pushkin, of Pestal, and of Ryleyof—those grand apostles of Sclavonian unity, conscience, order, and liberty.

The republicans of Spain hoped to establish free government upon the ruins of Bourbonism, but the effort was premature and failed. Neither the philosophy nor eloquence of Castellar, though coupled with the earnest zeal of able compatriots, was sufficient to secure success. These apostles of freedom should first have prepared the way for their gospel by enfranchising the religious faith of the masses. Individual thought and conscience should first have been awakened by the implanting of divine truth. The colporteur with his tracts and Testaments for the million, and the evangelist with an open Bible, should first have been called into the service of Spanish freedom. A free Bible and a free conscience, here as elsewhere, must become the heralds of political liberty. And this, in fact, inconsistent as it may appear with the public policy of Castellar, receives his earnest indorsement when he says: "If the Latin peoples could read—if they were obliged, at least every Sunday, to turn the pages of the Bible instead of hearing the chants of their priests in a strange and unutterable language, would they not have been two centuries ago republican?" "Because," he says, "the Bible is full, from the first page to the last, I will not say of republican ideas, but certainly of republican sentiments, which, with their poetry, have greater influence among the people at present."

It is unphilosophical and impossible to successfully establish and maintain republican institutions until the public mind is spiritually enfranchised and thoroughly imbued with those moral and religious principles which God only has revealed in His written Word as the rule of human conduct. A republic from necessity must have a spiritual prototype in the hearts of the masses, or else its existence at best will be but feeble and but a burlesque upon free government.

If those representative agitators of republican ideas, Kossuth, Mazzina, and Garibaldi, had in the beginning but assumed, as their life-work in the great drama of political reform, the sublime apostolate of the Cross, laboring first to give the Old World a true faith and a true conscience, Europe now, instead of suffering the pangs of premature political births, might feel the mighty movings of embryonic empires, whose timely advent would be hailed as an apocalypse of liberty by a generation born, not only to be free, but to establish and to maintain freedom; writing, if it need be, its sublime statutes by the light of battles and with the blood of martyrdom.

Garibaldi, to his credit, did, in his great scheme of Unification, comprehending the potency of divine revelation in emancipating the public mind, scatter throughout Italy his brief *foliums* or scriptural fragments, as an essential preliminary in the struggle with Ecclesiasticism for national unity and independence. And it is primarily to the influence of this stroke of spiritual and political philosophy that Garibaldi owes, in part, his prominence, and Italy her freedom from priestly thraldom.

With the truths of the Bible thoroughly interwoven

in the beginning into the faith of the people, these reformers might have laid the foundation upon which popular government, in due time, would have arisen in defiance of despotism. There is more latent military energy to be marshalled in behalf of freedom in a single copy of God's Word than there is in a whole squadron of enslaved or materialistic bayonets. It was the influence of a single Bible that awoke the spirit of the Reformation; that crippled the power of Rome; that drove back the arms of Charles—forcing his abdication; that wrested the Netherlands from the empire of Philip; that saved Protestant liberty on the field of Leutzan; that under Cromwell laid the foundation of English commerce and power; that for ever made grand and immortal through the Covenanter the memory of the Scot; that gave to the West a great empire of freedom, and that has finally impelled Anglo-Saxon language and law—those great missionaries of thought, liberty, and order—over half the globe. When the European liberalist accepts, as a political axiom of universal application, the faith of John Owen, that "The Bible is England's best hope," then he will comprehend the true philosophy of founding free government, and republicanism, as a necessary result, will, in the end, advance to universal supremacy.

The "United States of Europe," of which the republican theorist now dreams, will only assume promise and tangibility when the Bible shall have become a sacred and universal heir-loom with the cottager—when its poetry, its ethics, and its spiritual revelations shall have inspired the emotions, refined the morality, and sublimated the faith of the now stolid, down-trodden, priest-ridden masses. This great truth is forcibly exemplified in our own history. The century next preceding the formation of the Republic may justly be denominated the religious epoch—literally, the period of the Bible—the heroic period, out of which sprang the Revolution and constitutional liberty. Under colonial *regime* the Bible found a place in every family and school; and from this, more than from any other cause, came our declaration of rights, which not only focalized the holiest aspirations of all preceding ages, but which gave to freedom an impulse that will thrill all the ages of the future. So important was the Inspired Word considered in the maintaining of self-government in our early history that the Congress of 1777, on grounds of political and moral necessity, ordered the printing and circulation among the people of 20,000 copies of the Scriptures. And the Congress of 1781, for the same reasons, ordered for public use 30,000 copies more.

And here it is, in this early national faith in God's word, rather than in the abstract wisdom of statesmen or the genius of martial leaders, that rests the primary cause of our national progress. The heroes of the Revolutionary tribune and battle-field were but the consequent, the inevitable offspring of an historic period, which, under the procreative and quickening influences of the Divine Word, pulsated and glowed with heroic life. That epoch could have produced none others than heroes; could have produced no results other than the establishing of constitutional liberty. As the legendary angel of the Talmud visits and inspires the unborn child, so did the angel of the Word visit the unborn nation, and touched its heart, not only with an irrepressible love of freedom, but with the unconquerable energies of revolution. By this moral light we were ushered into the family of nations, and unconsciously guided through the political wilderness of the theoretic—were unconsciously directed over untrodden and unknown paths in our first efforts to demonstrate the new problem of government. And it was our Bibles, remotely inspiring the popular heart with the sublime equities of the Higher Law and the daring of a lofty faith, that finally snapped as ropes of sand the old thralls of party servitude, and brought, in the twinkling of an eye, the great North to its feet to meet in solid column the advance of the slave power. It was the silent forces of the Divine Word, coming up with the seeming might and majesty of Omnipotence through nearly two hundred years of colonial and national life, that made invincible the arms of freedom at Gettysburg, Antietam, Shiloh, and Lookout Mountain, and that finally, in the hour of the nation's triumph, drawing a veil over the examples of history, extended to the conquered the olive-branch instead of the sword—the fraternal welcome instead of the avenging statute.

So long as the Bible directs the popular conscience, so long will popular liberty with us remain impregnable. But whenever the American people put from them this great moral educator, and renounce the early faith of the Republic, then will have commenced a political decline which has, perhaps, in Gibbon or Bulwer an historic parallel. And as we comprehend this, who, I ask, is not startled with the thought, in view of the religious, moral, and political delinquencies of the hour, that this national renunciation may not already in effect have been proclaimed, and a consequent decline may not have even now commenced? Certain it is, the Bible has no longer that hold upon the reverence and affections of the masses it once had. And certain is it, that that firm religious trust, that rigid moral rectitude, that stern and simple virtue, which so distinguished the nation in its heroic and most republican days, is no longer a prominent trait. And also certain is it that that same social and moral condition which has invariably preceded the decay of other commonwealths is now being established with us.

The simple manners and rigid virtues of the generation of men who made Marathon, Salamis, and Platea immortal were lost in the luxurious ages of Cimon and of Periclese. With the influx of wealth from conquest, from tribute, and from the mines of Thasos and of Laurion, came luxury, vulgar ostentation, coarse sensuality, public extravagance, official corruption, and then the decline of Grecian liberty.

Private and public virtue gave Rome laws, wealth, and power, but the abuse of these gave her Cæsar, Nero, the Pretarian Guards, and then the Barbarians.

No close observer of the times, familiar with history and the indissoluble relations between free government and sound morality, can deny that our institutions are threatened with danger. Human nature, fundamentally, has experienced no perceptible change with the progress of the centuries. Two hundred years of unparalleled moral and political discipline have in no way modified the innate love of individual aggrandizement and power, even in the American heart. Catalines and Cæsars are to-day in our midst, in the garb of the most meek citizens of the Republic. The tyrant is ever present with us, waiting, unconsciously though it may be, the opportunity down the scale of national decadence, to measure and fix upon our soil the boundaries of his empire. So sure as it is that God's moral law is immutable—is still supreme throughout the conscious universe—is still the great Code by which we are to be governed in the maintaining of social order and of political liberty—so sure is it that, unless there is a tightening of moral bonds, a restraining of individual and public excesses in the use of wealth, privilege, and power, and a harmonizing of our life with the philosophy of the Divine Word, we are destined, at no remote period, to reach a point in our history at which liberty of conscience and of political sentiment will cease to exist as cardinal features of our government. This is no creation of morbid fancy, but is the solemn declaration of history, the inevitable deduction of philosophy, and the prophecy of an inspired faith. The astronomer can, with no more exactitude, predict an eclipse, the return of a periodic comet, or of a variable sun, than can the political philosopher determine the final result of the moral and religious sentiments of a people. Law extends its scepter over nations, as well as over worlds, determining their orbits, their influences, and their destiny.

And it is in the presence of this danger that we are led to appreciate the importance, in the preservation of republican institutions, of a spiritualized, vigilant, and aggressive Christian Church—that we perceive the true relations which exist between Church and State; that the problem of religious and political unity with us passes to a satisfactory solution.

The Bible, the great conservator of morals and of law, as well as the grand primordial in the establishing of our government, is a special trust of the Church.

And, as such, its truths become popularized and interwoven into the public faith in exact proportion to the fidelity with which that trust is discharged. If true to her obligations, the Church, through the citizen, becomes the sure support and hope of the State, vitalizing every pulsation and enriching every current of its life with that moral sense and moral force which, with the certainty of natural law, not only secures personal right, but gives to the Republic material wealth, social grandeur, and civil security. Not that the church, as an organization, should assume, or attempt to assume, a single prerogative of State, but should, through her teachings, impress upon the popular heart the great principles of God's Revealed Law. Through the religious sentiments of the nation, she should refine its ethics, purify its passions, invigorate its intellect, inspire its laws, unify its sympathies, and thereby build about its liberties an impregnable bulwark. That the Church is subject to arraignment for neglect of duty here cannot be denied. Existing facts testify too loudly against her. The moral and social desolations of the period convict her of serious delinquencies.

The spread of infidelity, the steady growth of licentiousness, the despotism of wealth and threatened revenges of labor, the decline of republican virtue and of private and public integrity, are living records of her recreancy. Perpetually are the melancholy testimonies of her guilt coming up from the cells of prisons, the dens of crime, the hovels of distress, the palaces of dissipation, the tribunals of perverted justice, the halls of venal legislation, the mercenary presence of executive power, and even from the very shadows of her own altars.

Individual and public morality, personal comfort, popular intelligence, pecuniary independence of the masses, and the equity of statutory laws, constitute the spiritual thermometer which indicates the zeal and fidelity of Christ's people. If chastity is a distinguishing trait; if laws are just and are faithfully observed; if honor in the commercial and political scales has more gravity than gold; if charity extends impartially her loving hands to the unfortunate; if industry and gold unite in the promotion of human comfort; if the decalogue is wrought into the consciences of the masses, then we may know that the Church is upon her knees; that upon her forehead is streaming the light of God; that upon her lips are glowing those immortal truths which have come down from lawgiver and prophet, Messiah and apostle, for the refining and the enfranchising of the world. But if hearthstones are breaking; if Sabbaths are forgotten; if prisons are crowded; if laws are unjust; if wealth supplants virtue and poverty becomes a synonym for crime; if gold plants its jeweled heel upon the heart of labor, and, in expiation, builds costly altars to the Most High; if immorality taints the atmosphere of private and public life; if the pulpit becomes enervated, and ceases its fearless criticisms, its fiery threatenings, and its sacred individuality becomes involved in the whirl of luxury and of worldly excitement—then we may know the Church is recreant to her trust; that infidelity has chilled her faith, and that indolence and ease are more congenial to her tastes than are those toils and sufferings, those self-denials and disinterested loves which have ever been and which ever will be the only sygnets of her fidelity, the only gems that will sparkle in her coronet in that great day when her mission is complete and the world passes to final judgment.

And is it difficult to determine the spiritual condition of the Church to-day, guided by these evidences? Are our homes, as a rule, eminent nurseries of the good, the true, and the lofty in character? Are they moral castles, strong and impregnable in their walls and their towers? Do their fires never die out with those who in love kindled them, and who in unity nourished them? Go to the records of our courts, and there read of the desolation of firesides, of the wrecks of sacred hopes, of the sundering of tender ties, of the sorrows of helpless offspring, and then answer. Are our Sabbaths held in sacred remembrance and revered as holy because of the commands of God and the wants of humanity? Go stand on that day upon the thoroughfares and at the outlets of our cities and towns, and listen to the roll of the drum, the blare of the trumpet, and the shouts of the returning mob. Go out upon your streets at the hour of Sabbath evening hymn and witness the crowded vestibules of your theatres, the brilliant and thronged saloon, the dimly-lighted but packed, mephitic, subterranean dance-rooms that everywhere allure to fascinate, unbalance, and overthrow your sons and your neighbors, and then answer. Are our jails and penitentiaries decreasing and becoming tenantless? Go visit our seats of government, and there examine the constantly-augmenting appropriations for their extension and support, and then answer. Does wealth hide no moral deformities; does it never seduce the heart and steal the homage due to virtue? Is even honest poverty more a misfortune than an aggravated crime? Go into all the walks of life—upon the streets, into the public assembly, the halls of justice, and even into the sanctuary of prayer, and there witness the license allowed to wealth—the deference, the partialities, and the slavish obsequiousness so anxiously paid to gold, and then answer. Is the social atmosphere free from moral taints that poison and wither the greenest and holiest of human fruitage? Go into the retirements of domestic life, and there glance over the columns and cuts of the periodicals which too often find welcome from under the pens and pencils of perverted genius, and then answer. Do the pulpits and the press of the Church fill the land with their voices; reaching all the by-ways and dark recesses of human misery with their prophetic words of warning, their tender accents of sympathy, their anxious pleadings for a higher life? Go into the abodes of luxury, into the hovels of poverty, into the haunts of crime, and there mark as a rule either the absolute religious solitude, or, at best, only the faint and occasional echoes of an equivocal and unimpassioned appeal from these ministers of Christ, and then answer. Do these assumed advocates of a beneficent gospel as fearlessly espouse the cause of the poor, in their unequal struggle with wealth and power, as of the opulent? Go listen to the pathetic recitals of the weak; to the sighs of overworked, ill-paid labor, as it rises, with aching heart and tired limb, to toil through the long hours in the vitiated atmosphere of the task-room, or in the sweltering sun, or pitiless storm, that mere shelter, bread, and garments may be won for the waiting, patient companions of a dwarfed and cheerless life, and then answer.

Do these assumed tribunes of divine equity as boldly attack crime in the purple as in the garb of the peasant? Go to the cells of the prison and there see only, as a rule, the victims either of a moral or a social necessity; those upon whom in the cradle, and even in the womb, has only fallen a darkened moral light, or upon whom the remorseless hand of penury, revenge, or of seeming fate, has heavily rested; while the tinseled, dramatic actor of stupendous crime is still free to sneer at courts and juries, at divine injunctions, at human virtues, and to build about him still higher and higher his impregnable bulwarks of gold, and then answer. Do the hands of ordination always fall upon those worthy of being denominated "stars in the right hand of Christ;" worthy of the mantle of such as Knox, Luther, Edwards, Wesley, Asbury, McKendree, and others of the great apostolic line, with whom self-denial, toil, suffering, and even death were welcome, if for the glory of the cross and the amelioration of human want? Go lift the curtain that hides the interior life of some of our clergy mark their leanings toward the materialism of the Tyndalls, of the Spencers, or of the Huxleys; their gravitations toward the utilitarianism of Hume, the psilanthropism of Channing, or the ritualism of Rome. Follow them out into the busy world, as they tread their way among the multitudes, along the avenues of worldly profit, into the great highways of speculation, crossing even the threshold of the Stock Exchange, that arena of chance and of guilded fraud, so ghastly with the wrecks of fortune, of honor, of life, and of a future hope, and there witness in the priestly heart its consuming greed, its fireless altar, its dead Urim and Thummim, and then answer. Truly, the emergencies of the hour call for a more self-abnegating, a more enthusiastic, a more aggressive and comprehensive spirit at the great centres of religious force. From these sources of power an influence should go forth which would pervade the entire social being of the Republic; vitalizing its conscience, quickening its faith, and inspiring all its activities with a stern and sublime rectitude. When that great Catholic Missionary, Francis Xavier, was on the eve of departure for India, he was shown in dreams of the night the fields he was to win to the Truth. Vast continents, islands, and empires which he was to conquer to the "Holy Faith" arose, one after another, upon his vision like a retinue of unlighted worlds; and yet, in the fervor of his religious zeal and infinity of his apostolic ambition, he exclaimed, "Yet more, O my God! yet more!" And such should be the zeal of every herald of the Cross in these days of decaying faith. The cry of Xavier, "Yet more, O my God! yet more!" should echo from every consecrated lip until the great heart of the nation would pulsate in rythmic harmony with the pure and sublime spirit of the Divine Logos.

To-day, even, the Church, like a dumb and paralytic prophet under the weight of Divine displeasure, is sitting in the midst only of a splendid barbarism. The ideal civilization of the Christian is still in the womb of the future. It is not enough that we as a people theoretically assume the Christian faith; that we stamp "God" upon our coin, or incorporate the sacred name into our Constitution. It is not enough that we build costly houses of worship and swing their doors to the comfortably-fed and comfortably-clad; that we found schools in the name of freedom and yet refuse the child its sacred creed. It is not enough that we give by proxy to the poor and formally bury the pauper in the name of the Lord; that we ordain public humiliations and fasts, national thanksgivings and prayer. It is not enough that we plant our faith by the Ganges, the Yang-tse-Kiang, the Nile, and upon the islands of the sea. Rome, the mother of popular ignorance, of intolerance, and of want, can boast of all this, even upon a broader and a grander scale. Constantine and his barbaric legions with equal right boasted of the Christian faith upon the plea that they bore its symbol upon their banners and their shields, carrying it as the ensign of ambitious conquest. Something more than this is needed to develop into symmetrical proportion the moral, social and political character of the nation. If we would build up into ideal strength and beauty the manhood and womanhood of the Republic, we must reach the inner life of the masses, arouse the public conscience, and touch all the springs of the divine and heroic in the great popular heart.

To accomplish this, however, there must be a systematic, an energetic, unremitting, universal effort. No violent, spasmodic local outburst of public virtue will alone avail. The moral lapse is too great, too widely-spread to admit of any course but that which shall thoroughly and permanently improve and inspire the fundamental forces of life. As the Roman hierarchy plans and labors, not for this alone, but for the coming centuries, so should the true Church, by a uniform, constant, and persistent effort, labor to build up and mould the personality of the nation into forms of ethic and civic beauty. If the Church would fully perform her obligations, preserving with all civil and religious liberty inviolate, she must radically change her agents and modes of popular education. In these days of steam and of electricity, when thought multiplies with the moments to infinity, and flashes over the latitudes and longitudes with the speed of lightning, she must seize upon some other agents or fulcrums of power than simply her pulpits and her present literature to move and inspire the world. Were she fully awake to her responsibilities; were she intelligently and conscientiously earnest in intensifying her rightful influence, and in extending and solidifying her moral empire, she would readily discover the means which are now presented to her for the fulfillment of this work. From the impulses of free thought, and the necessities of free government, the common school, and from the evolutions of genius, the steam-press with its daily newspaper, have appeared as the most potent agents for the dissemination of popular thought and inspiration.

The pulpit and the library, as moral educators of the masses, are of the old dispensation. These are of the new—the dispensation of universal mental quickening—of restless, independent thought; and by these the destiny of our political, social, and religious life is to be mainly determined. As these are inspired so will our national character be formed and our national history written.

And yet the Church, practically, is insensible to this. She seems to be sleeping with contentment upon the old flint-locks of the Revolution, while the restless age, without prophet or Messiah, is wielding the Columbiads and rifle-guns which Providence has expressly prepared for the successful completion of her own conquests.

The circumscribed and periodic duties of the sacred desk; eccentric expositions of divine truth; denominational aggrandizement the building of ostentatious altars; the inauguration of fanatical temperance crusades; the issue of feeble weekly sectarian journals, and the effort to renew races and civilizations long since effete by fulfillment of appointed time, seems to fill the very measure of her ambition and her hopes.

An effective externality is seemingly the grand sum of her desires. Figuratively, the apostolic zeal and simplicity of teaching, healing, and inspiring by the wayside, and in the chambers of the poor and lowly, are apparently of far less moment than are the ostentatious environments, the awe-inspiring rites and ceremonies of the temple.

When she will arouse to a consciousness of her responsibility, and with a fresh baptism and a broader vision commence a new era of struggle with antiChrist, striking at the foundations of evil rather than at results, is a sealed problem. Judging, however, from her present secularistic tendencies, we fear that around her altars must first sweep cyclones whose fury will not only threaten her own safety but that of the Republic. The signs of the times significantly point to this. It requires no prophetic ear to even now catch the sobs of the coming storm.

Materialism, under the teachings of the Pantheistic scientists; politico-ecclesiasticism, the star of Papal hope; imperialism, the ideal polity of vulgar affluence; monopoly, the ambitious aim of Jesuitical wealth; agrarianism, the defined and settled theory of the Communist; free-love, the apotheosis of socialism; with their concomitants, are spreading and entrenching themselves in every direction, preparatory to a struggle for supremacy. In results, the mightiest conflict of all certainty of ideas is surely approaching—a conflict in which Christianity and republican government upon this continent will either become more clearly defined and more deeply rooted, or else will, for a time at least, relapse into simple ideals; having no tangible form or force in law.

In the face of existing facts, this crisis should not only become an absorbing desire with the Church, but its approach she could hasten; for its speedy advent is the grand hope of constitutional and religious freedom. Delay can only increase the intensity of the struggle and the chances of success.

Material prosperity and prolonged rest have stricken the Church with the weakness of senility; and therefore some great struggle, in whose surges her fortunes shall tremble and vibrate with dread uncertainty, is her first and greatest need. It is a necessity of being, applicable to collective as well as to individual life, that the perfect, the ideal good shall only be reached and maintained through conflict and suffering. The faith of the Church has ever been most mighty, her glory most resplendent, when the foe has pressed most heavily upon her flanks. It was only when the chariots of the Egyptian were thundering at the heels of Israel that the sea parted to his footsteps, and the "pillar of cloud and of fire" stood between the oppressor and the freedman.

It was because of impending danger to the Hebrew Church that, for more than four hundred years, the invisible battalions of God formed its imperial guard. And so have been the sublimest periods of the Church of Christ when the sword and the fagot have most scourged her ranks; when the caves and the fastnesses of the mountains have most echoed her plaintive chants and prayers. These were the days of her real transfiguration; the days of her true scriptural simplicity and of her greatest spiritual ardor. Not that we would have a repetition of this sad history, for this was the sorrow of conditions never to return —the sorrow of a rude age, of a numerical weakness —a discipline necessary to the deep implanting and final growth of a lofty and sturdy faith. But we would have her, in these days of her material plentitude and of her spiritual poverty, forced into some great moral conflict, whose uncertainties would startle her dreams, quicken her pulse, sublimate her faith, and lead her into closer communion with her celesial allies.

In a period like this, civilization and free law would catch a new inspiration, and march upward with colossal strides toward grander heights. That the penalties of neglected duties and of perverted laws may be alleviated the Christian element of the nation, in its civil capacity, either united or in its denominational character, should at once move on the line of the aggressive, and take position at the great points of moral strength.

In the military campaigns of Napoleon, aggression, combined with celerity of action, was the grand characteristic that gave to his arms victory and empire. Aggression embodies force that mere numbers do not alone possess. This should be a leading feature in the policy of the Church. Though theoretically peaceful, yet she should become aggressive, and move without delay, figuratively with her hand upon her sword-hilt, to control not only the daily press of the nation, but to place the Bible in its schools as a text-book of moral and political inspiration. Here we indicate the great work of the future—the grandest of the age—and point to a battle-field upon which the Christian Church, in her individuality, must finally carry her standards, though it be in the face of relentless storm and opposition. The struggle she may postpone, but its coming is inevitable; for in that struggle only is now hope of political and social reform, as well as that of her own regeneration. The fiery crucible is still indispensable in the reforming and refining of nations, of the Church, and of the individual man. Surely her surpliced bishops, and her meek-mannered ministers must finally, alike, if loyal to their trusts, throw off their robes of peace, and, war-clad and fearless as were Luther, Knox, and Wesley, lead in striking for the triumphs of a national conscience and a national faith, which shall give consistency to our public acts, and no longer contradict our professions of Christian ethics.

The preliminary steps should be a unification of evangelical strength for all public measures of moral and social good; among the chief of which should be the establishing of daily newspapers at the great centres of population and of influence, of such a character and at such a cost as would defy all competition, and thereby be enabled to carry, in the true spirit of the missionary, to every fire-side, however humble or impoverished, a daily resume of the world's enterprises, industries, charities, aims, triumphs in science and in faith, as well as to inspire and aid Labor in its unequal struggle for competency and independence; leaving the history of the passions now so prominently presented, and so potent in the work of demoralization, unwritten, except as judicial records. This is entirely feasible if earnestly and judiciously undertaken. The money even that is now annually expended in the extravagant construction and appointments of edifices of worship; in the maintaining of an abortive system of sectarian journalism; in the support under existing circumstances of a questionable economy of foreign missions; in the personal extravagance of professing Christians, would alone successfully establish a journalistic influence scarcely secondary to that of all the leading dailies of the country combined—certainly an influence which, if wielded with sagacity and fidelity, would send an ethic glow, now unfelt and unknown, through all the arteries, and along all the nerves of the body politic.

The "Centennial Fund" of the Methodist Episcopal Church North amounted to $5,000,000 — a sum sufficient to have successfully established three powerful dailies, either of which might have possessed a popular influence that would have far transcended that of the great "Book Concern" of this denomination, with its thirty cylinder power-presses—combined even with the 25,000 preachers and 1,000 instructors in the colleges and seminaries of this sect.

The Baptists now contemplate the collection of a similar fund; but it is hoped, if successful, the moral and social education of the masses, especially that element in which Communism is striking deep and luxuriant root, and which forms so large a proportion of the numerical and vital power of the nation, may be liberally provided for by their sect in the establishing of a powerful daily press.

Moral, social, and political science is infinitely of more national importance than theology, rhetoric, and the Pagan classics. Teach the masses, conjointly

with the rudiments of secular education, the sanctity
of the moral law, the divinity of the eleventh commandment, and political economy, and we lay deep—
the foundation of popular sovereignty and build about
it a bulwark, over which the ambitions of a secularized priesthood, of jesuitical monopolies, of political
demagogues, and of social iconoclasts can never pass.

The denominational classes parade the results of
their sectarian enterprises in self-commendatory statistics of the number of their clergy, their theological
schools, their libraries, their periodicals and tracts;
but what are all their pulpits, their seminaries, their
fixed and periodical literature, in their direct popular
influence, compared with that of the daily press?
While their voices only reach, at indefinite, or at best
at weekly or semi-weekly periods, the disciplined and
comfortable thousands, the daily press may reach, not
only these, but all the unbridled and needy millions.
This is the great arch-apostle of our century, speaking with infinite tongues of infinite power. In its
nervous and eternal syllables is embodied a force more
mighty, if free, than that of armies—a force in whose
flash, crowns, bayonets, senates, statutes, creeds, organizations, and men, melt and pass away. Give the
" Nazarine" the daily press, and the fortress is gained
whose guns command the world. Rescue it from its
lawless and mercenary condition, sanctify it to the just,
the pure, and the lofty, and we not only encourage
the advance to the political front, over the heads of
demagogues, the " honest, capable, and faithful," but
we embody in one the equivalent of all the diversified
moral and intellectual power of the past as well as of
the present. We may even gather up from sacred
dust into single quivers, as arrows of quenched light,

the long spent forces of genius, and send them out again in perpetual streams, rekindled and reinspired, over broader and vaster circuits; making the Chrysostoms and the Abelards, the Luthers and the Fenelons, the Sydneys and the Miltons, the Whitfields and the Chathams, the Masillons and the Turgots, the Adamses and the Franklins, speak again, in grander and more intensified periods, to grander and more intensified audiences. "The newspaper," said Lord Mansfield, "will write the Dukes of Northumberland out of their titles and possessions, and the country out of its king." "Before this century shall have run out," said Lamartine, "journalism will be the whole of human thought. * * * * * * The ruling book, possibly, will be a daily newspaper." The financial and political centers of all Europe thrill as sensitively in response to the leaders of the *London Times* as do the magnets of our planet in response to the solar storm. And does not the religious world see its fearful responsibility here involved in neglecting to control this mighty agent of social and political power—this agent by which civilization and all the sacred interests of the race are to receive their ultimate type—their final cast?

Better worship beneath humble roof and beside lowly altar, and know that through our zeal and our sacrifices we are hewing the great rough block of sensual humanity into the beauty of divine proportion, and gradually bringing into being the grand ideal of Christian hope and of popular liberty.

Ascendancy gained in journalism, then, should follow an effort to restore the Bible to the common schools. But here we approach a field of earnest conflict, a field upon which forces, now quietly strengthening and intensifying at the foundations of society, will finally rally for supremacy. What the arbitrament, however, of that field will be need not be a question of doubt. With the influence of the Press and the inspiration of the cause no friend of Christian civilization and of popular government need stumble in his conclusions, or bow himself in fear. I am aware, however, that there exists, even with some of the assumed friends of the Bible, objections to its introduction into the public schools. Influenced by denominational sympathies, and lacking a just comprehension of the political necessity, the scope, and the national pre-eminence of the common school, they advise against its introduction there, excusing their sectarian prejudice and their virtual disloyalty to the State, as well as to the Bible, in appeals for "independent" or denominational schools. While others, moved by fear of the opposition which the effort of introduction would provoke, are led to tamely submit to its exclusion, choosing peace with no Bible rather than the social and political contests which would follow. But to thus yield up our great system of public instruction into the hands of demagogues, to the control of hereditary enemies of popular government and of social order, without a struggle, is not only an act of cowardice, but a crime against liberty; a crime that will finally bring, alike upon Church and State, overwhelming disaster.

That the effort would invoke strenuous opposition we have no doubt, but shall we refuse to attempt so plain a duty because of opposition? Can we elect in this matter? Is not the introduction of the Inspired Word into our schools a necessity which we, as guardians of free government, must accept at all hazards? Is this not a required evidence of the necessary moral rectitude essential to the successful maintenance of self-government?

By legal enactment we seek to establish our faith, to lull the public conscience, and to dignify the national character by engraving "In God we trust" upon our coin, and by incorporating into our organic law a more specific declaration of our faith. But is this sufficient? Would it not be more consistent with our religious assumptions to place the Bible in our schools, and thereby seek to engrave upon the hearts of our children a declaration of our trust, in lines more deep and more imperishable than they can be upon our coin or our organic acts? It was not sufficient with God that the Hebrews should simply engrave His name and His words upon their doorposts and their gates; but it was upon the hearts of their children that He especially designed that His statutes should be written; for it was here that He was to establish, not alone Hebrew government, but to lay the foundations of prophetic civilization. And so should we, imitating the Jews in their obedience, not alone seek to write our faith upon mere gold or parchment, but to incorporate it into our system of public instruction, and thereby figuratively bind it as a sign upon the hands of the national childhood, and as frontlets between its eyes.

No plea, however specious, no portrayal of danger, however threatening, can be of sufficient force to warrant a prohibition of the use of the Bible in the public schools. Its presence there is the imperious demand of moral, social, and political progress. Our system of common schools is no result of Pantheism, Paganism, Vaticanism, or even of Judaism. No such scheme of education was ever born of these mothers of Anti-Christ. Each has had ages of empire. Each has stamped its genius upon the centuries; and yet they give us no record of a system of free education for the great laboring, patient, needy masses. This is the peculiar offspring of the Christianized American idea of social and political necessity—that grand idea of conscience and of liberty which had its conception in the religious inspirations of the sixteenth century — embryonic life in the early experiences of the Puritans, and birth in the cabin of the *Mayflower*. No priest of Jerusalem or of Rome, no disciple of Heroclitus or of Lucretius, no forerunner of Voltaire, Hume, or of Hegal stood sponsor at the baptism of our cherished system of schools. None but the saintly " Pilgrim," with his Bible and his " hymns of lofty cheer," was there to give pledge for this offering of Christian liberty. And why, then, should we yield to the dictates of these foes of Christian revelation, and as a logical historic sequence of popular government? What principles of duty, necessity, or expediency demand this? Are our institutions so deeply entrenched that we can, as a mark of republican generosity, for any reason, safely hand them over to the control of their natural enemies? Or can we, in the *role* of the demagogue, afford, even for a season, to barter this or any guaranty of our liberties for place or emolument?

> "Oh! not yet
> Mayest thou embrace thy corselet, nor lay by
> Thy sword, nor yet, O Freedom! close thy lids
> In slumber; for thine enemy never sleeps,
> And thou must watch and combat, till the day
> Of the new Earth and Heaven." BRYANT.

The most momentous reasons exist why the Scriptures should be introduced into the schools as a text-book of ethics. Never since the great flood of Gothic and Vandal life which rushed over the Alps in the early centuries has there been such a flow of peoples as is now setting in upon us from the old seats of European and Asiatic civilizations. Irresistible and ceaseless is this tide of vitality now flowing to our shores, with all its crude ideas of religion, of morals, and of government; vitiating more and more the republican sentiment of the nation, as each succeeding wave, sweeping over the land, leaves in its broad continental track the germs of new life, the elements of new power. The historic Roman disappeared beneath the great northern deluge; because he not only lacked the moral power to resist and to assimilate the vigorous barbarism that flowed in upon him, but the means to secure it. So is the historic American gradually losing his individuality and power amidst the great deluge of the east and the west.

With this type came liberty; and with its extinction liberty will expire, unless its spirit and its personality are perpetuated through those who are now succeeding to political duty and responsibility. Unlike the Roman, however, we possess the means not only to resist, but to assimilate all these elements of antagonism which surround us with such gloomy promise. With the Bible inspiring the statute, the tribune, the press, and the school, we may mold all this mighty influx of Paganism, Romanism, Atheism, and Communism into our own likeness; making it a part of ourselves in the hopes and perpetuity of the Republic.

Can any doubt this? Can any doubt the power of Christian philosophy in resisting, overcoming, and finally assimilating antagonistic elements to itself when faithfully taught and exemplified? If so, we have only to refer to its early struggles and final triumphs to fully comprehend this truth. No other proofs are wanted to establish forever its irresistible energy as an agent of defense, of reform, of conquest, and of empire, than its early struggles with, and its decisive victories over, old-established and venerated creeds and systems of philosophy, with which it first came in contact when only exemplified in the teachings and lives of but even a little band of humble Galileans. Old and deep as were the foundations of the ritualism of the Jew, lofty and unyielding as was the intellectual pride of the Greek, imperial and splendid as was the barbarism of the Roman, beautiful and enslaving as was the mythology of the classic Pagan, these, all these, were shaken and overthrown by the gentle, but yet irresistible and revolutionary spirit of that philosophy which Jesus so meekly taught to men, and which His disciples so faithfully expounded, not only to the Jew, but to the Gentile, at Athens, at Corinth, and at Rome. And its modern victories are no less convincing of its powers than are those of its early history. It may sometimes, in subordination to the great law of reaction, appear for a time to have lost its vitality and power; but like the eternal flow of the tides, inflow follows outflow, and each succeeding wave lifts the social life-line higher and higher, and will until the highest summits of human possibilities are reached, and, in fulfillment of the great drama, the finite blends with the shadow of the Infinite.

Napoleon said: " Alexander, Cæsar, Charlemagne, and myself have founded empires; but upon what does the creation of our genius rest? Upon force," he replies. "Christ," he continues, "founded His empire upon love, and millions at this hour would die for Him. I see kings, potentates, and armies arrayed against Him; but with Him I see no army—none but a mysterious force—peaceful men, scattered here and there, having no rallying-point but a common faith in the mysteries of the Cross. I die before my time, and my empire expires with me; but the Kingdom of Christ survived the Crucifixion; still lives, extending its scepter over the earth."

Our success in assimilating the great mass of this rapidly inflowing alien element, as well as in perpetuating the true republican spirit with the native-born, will be mainly determined by the ethic forces we employ in our educational system. If our agents of conversion and of perpetuation are wanting in the requisite power to inspire and to elevate the moral sentiments, then we shall fail in our work. But if we bring to our aid influences which, by their natural adaptation and their spiritual force, incite and develop the emotional nature into pure and lofty types, as well as stimulate the understanding, then our success will equal our hopes. And here exists an unfortunate point of difference among even the stanch friends of our public schools. While some, overlooking the need of Christian ethic culture as a political and social necessity, maintain that a system of public instruction, purely secular, is all that is required in laying the foundation of republican citizenship, others contend that secular studies, alone, possess no inherent influence especially favorable to republican sentiment; that it is only through the emotions, guided by an enlightened understanding, that we can build up a strong and systematic republican character. Hence, they claim that, on political grounds alone, the Bible, so prepotent in its power over the heart in restraining and refining its passions, in quickening the conscience, and in inspiring the mind with the true ideas of equity and of equality, should be introduced into the public schools as a reading-book, that the great moral deficiency which exists in the popular character, through the negligence or recreancy of the guardian, may be at least partially supplied by the State.

That the position of the latter is correct we have abundant proof. It is not the merely intellectually trained that have proved the exclusive champions or the most sturdy defenders of republican principles. It was not from the scholarly and courtly ranks of England that chiefly came the most strong and ardent supporters of the commonwealth, but it was from the fields and the shops—from the industrial ranks of the lowly and emotional Puritans, that sprang, as if by inspiration, those fiery and invincible squadrons of republicanism. It was not from schools of classic learning that mainly flowed the heroic spirit of the American Revolution, but it was from the counting-rooms, the workshops, and the farms, recruited from common schools with Bibles, that gathered those untrained battalions who sealed with unutterable sorrows their devotion to liberty, and won for humanity its first substantial victory.

Russell and Sydney are conspicuous among the martyrs of English liberty. Their republican sympathies brought them to the scaffold. And the first extenuation of this crime against human rights came from the halls of Oxford. While the block was yet reeking with the blood of these martyrs of free thought Oxford University proclaimed to the world that the principles for which these men died were "impious; were damnable—doctrines fitted to deprave the manners and corrupt the minds of men; to promote sedition and to overthrow states."

Pure intellect, however highly cultivated, untempered with Christian philosophy, is inclined to inordinate self-devotion or to caste, and is, therefore, instinctively antagonistic to popular sovereignty.

The American Republic struggled into life in the midst of a brilliantly intellectual age — the age of Bentham and of Herschell; of d'Alembert and of Condillac; of Kant and of Lossing; of Goethe and of Schiller; and yet, scarcely any great intellect, save Chatham, Barre, and Burke, rose up in that splendid period of philosophy, poetry, eloquence, and of law, to inspire, even with hope, the founders of the infant Republic. The ostentatious reception of the American Ambassador by the savans and literati of France, in 1778, was the result more of national prejudice against England than from true love of republicanism. The kiss of Voltaire and of Franklin, as symbolical of political sympathy, in the presence of the imperial intellect of France, was dramatic, overwrought, and unnatural, and no more represented a unity of political inspiration than did the great revolutions of the two peoples. Truly, republics have ever been born of the heart, christened by its affections, and defended by its enthusiasm.

The public school, where the childhood of the nation daily gathers—where the great majorities of coming power meet to receive the first lesson of civic life—is the most effective point at which we can reach the faith and the conscience of the future. And it is here, then, that the Bible should be placed as a text-book of moral, social, and political inspiration. Sabbath-schools do not fully meet the necessities of the case, for reasons readily assigned. We do not presume, however, that the Bible in the schools would at once and alone work out the great problem of social and political science—would alone accomplish all for civil and religious freedom. Moral and civil treason would still continue. Tribunals of justice and prisons would still be needed as necessary adjuncts of our present civilization. For, with all the spiritual and moral appliances within human reach, the upward march of the race is, as is the march of the centuries, perceptible only by comparison of epochs or eras. To educate man up to the full standard of the Christian ideal, when statutes of force shall become obsolete, when individual right shall find impregnable defense in the right of another, is a work of ages — slow in its processes, it may be, as is the precession of the equinoxes. But with its presence there the pulse of the nation would beat stronger; its life would become grander; its step toward higher planes would be more sure and steady; because, with the Divine Word goes out an influence which mind, particularly in its formative period, cannot wholly resist. Silent and unostentatious as the light in its operations though it is, still, few hearts there are that can pass from under its continued influence without receiving some of the strokes of its divine sculpturing, or some of the touches of its divine coloring.

William Tyndall must have felt this when laboriously translating in exile the Word for the fatherland, desiring that it might be given even to every plow-boy of England. Faber felt it when he said, " The poetry and philosophy of the Bible live on the ear like music that never can be forgotten." Erasmus realized it when he wished that not only the "husbandman at the plow, but his little ones at the cottage-fire, might sing something from the Gospels and the Epistles." De Quincey was conscious of it when he said, "The Scriptures which I read in childhood ever sway me as mysteriously as music, and slept on my memory like early dawn upon the waters." Burke, Chatham, Erskine, Otis, Henry, Ames, Webster, and other great masters of language, early understood its mysterious power in giving resistless charm to eloquence and to argument. Elizabeth Fry had faith in its influence over the adult as well as youthful criminal, and had sublime confirmation of it when in the English prisons she recited its tender compassions, its sweet reconciliations, its inspiring hopes, and awoke within their gloomy walls a new and eloquent life. Gustavus, the knightly hero of Protestant liberty, fully comprehended, as did Cromwell, the power even of its martial influence, when, with his unhelmeted warriors, on the eve of battle, he would reverently plead its promises of help, and trustingly chant the hymns of its inspiration.

Freedom by the Danube, thrilled with divine hope, beneath the influence of Revelation, as Kossuth, kneeling amidst the graves of the heroes of Ranoyina, plead with inspired lips for the glory of the fallen brave and the cause of Hungarian liberty.

It was the imperial power of Christian Revelation that wrung from the apostate Julian that sublime confession when, upon the sands by the Tigris, flinging his own blood toward heaven, he exclaimed, "Galileean! Galileean! Thou hast conquered!"

We give to the public schools, as models of moral excellence, of diction, of pathos, and of the sublime,

Milton, Young, Dwight, Ruskin, Webster, Bryant, and other eminent teachers; but when these, as ethical standards, are viewed simply as reflexes of those inimitable lessons of the "humble Nazarine," how quickly do they lose their importance and take inferior rank in the realm of philosophy! What weakness of imagery do we find with these authors when paralleled with that which arose in the visions of John at Patmos, of Ezekiel by the Chebar, and of Daniel by the Euphrates! What passionless poetry when placed in the light of that which kindled upon the lips of Deborah, of Job, of David, and of Isaiah! What emotionless pathos, when contrasted with that which trembled in the voice of the prophet by the rivers of captivity, or when, down through the ages, lamenting, he saw the final scattering and exile of his people.

While the embodied thoughts and emotions of human teachers may, for a time, charm and thrill with their magnetic power, they quickly become spiritless and inert when compared with the written inspirations of Jehovah. The grandest and purest philosophy, the sublimest and most impassioned poetry, the boldest and most startling imagery, the loftiest and most enrapturing diction, the tenderest and most tearful pathos which ever thrilled the human heart, come from the pens of God's lawgivers—from the lips of God's prophets—from the harps of God's poets. It is at these sources of wondrous power that the great statesmen, orators, bards, and soldiers of reform have ever caught their inspiration, have ever kindled the torch with which they have spanned the heavens with the broadest and brightest arches of promise. And it is here that the great masters of immortal art have received their divinest inspirations of the beautiful, the grand, the tragic, and the awful.

Mythology was the inspiration of Greek art; hence, its apotheosis was simply beauty of form and fidelity of expression. But the Bible inspired the genius of the Renaissance, whose art creations embody not only beauty of line and of sentiment, but ideas, whose forces thrill the universe, and whose sweep touches the very heart of the Infinite.

If the " Minerva " of Phidias, the " Venus " of Praxitiles, the " Lance Bearer " of Polycletus, are perfections of ideal beauty, the marbles of Ghiberti, of Donotello, and of Canova, are but little less. But the infinite grandeurs and transcendencies of Michael Angelo, the sublimities and pathos of Raphael, the divine harmonies and purity of Coreggio, in their illustrations of the Messianic drama, have no parallel in the grandest of Pagan art. Toby Rosenthal at one time threw a portion of the artistic world into ecstacies in materializing " Elaine"—a conception of Tennyson; but this young Jewish master might call up with his magic pencil, from the grand old poetry of his own race, conceptions and ideals, in the light of which " Elaine " would pale like a star at midday. When this novel work of Rosenthal's shall have been forgotten, the sacred illustrations of even Gustave Doré will still live to inspire and rap the hearts of men.

We read of the great lyric power of the old Pagan masters; but critics decide, that while the cultivated music of the most distinguished of these was full of harmony and of tender melody, it was yet effeminate, and lacked vastly the variety of air and of modulation, the pathos, the power, and the grandeur of that of the

Christian. The celebrated *nomes* of Hyagnis, of Timotheus, and of Pindar, rendered in the temples at the zenith of Greek glory, deserve no comparison with the sublime oratorios of Handel, of Haydn, of Mozart, or of Gibbons. These choral symphonies, upon which so many millions in emotion have again and again swept into communion with the angelic choirs, could have had no creation except by inspiration of the Bible.

Emerson says Milton is forerun by Homer, Virgil, and Tasso; that without these precursors there would have been no "Paradise Lost." But Emerson here is superficial; dealing simply with the anatomy of poetry. Its spirit glows now, beyond the limit of his observation. Had there been no Iliad, no Æneid, or no Jerusalem Delivered, "Paradise Lost" would not have been; for it was an inevitable epic creation of the Inspired Word—a grand, irrepressible poetic out-burst of the faith of the Christian centuries. The forerunners of Milton were the Hebriac prophets and the Messianic revelators. And these will ever furnish epic and dramatic genius its most seraphic conceptions and its most imperishable models.

Milton declared that "no songs were comparable with the songs of the Bible, and no orations equal to the orations of the prophets."

Sir William Jones thought the "Scriptures contained more sublimity and more exquisite beauty than can be collected from all other books."

The learned and eloquent Herder said, "The poetry of the Bible is the most thrilling and sublime of all poetry."

Erasmus says, "Paul, at the close of the fourth Chapter of Romans, is more eloquent than Cicero."

Goethe pronounced the book of Ruth "the loveliest epic idyl that has come down from any age."

Humbolt asserted that "The Hebrew description of nature was unrivaled, and the 104th Psalm the sublimest panorama of the universe."

Carlyle remarks that " the book of Job is the grandest thing ever written—a noble book with sublime sorrow — sublime reconciliations; the oldest melody of the heart of manhood, * * * * * so soft, and great as the Summer midnight—as the world with its seas and stars."

" The elder Pitt recognized the Bible as " the criterion of political equity ; as the highest instrument of popular appeal when tyranny violated constitutional right ; and in it found justification for revolution when public liberty was assailed."

Burke acknowledged the power of the Bible in "inspiring public energy, and the spirit of popular liberty." And, upon the authority of his biographer, it was "from its pages that he imbibed that sublime morality, and gathered that rich imagery, apt illustrations, and lofty diction," which have made his orations classic and immortal.

Erskine said, " The principles taught by the Bible lay at the foundation of English laws ; and that under the auspices of the Inspired Word only had the lost and subverted liberties of mankind been re-asserted."

John Stuart Mill, that obdurate and subtle skeptic, in a candid moment, admits that what " Christian Revelation lacks in direct strength is more than compensated by the greater truth and rectitude of the morality it sanctions."

Guizot writes : " The nations who are conquering the world by mind and strength derive their mission and their source of power from the Bible."

Victor Hugo says: "England made Shakspeare, and the Bible made England."

Samuel Adams declared "The Holy Word the only infallible guide in morals and religion — the palladium of the rights of conscience, of liberty, and of happiness."

Out of the "great idea of God's infinite attributes, as revealed in His Word," Theodore Parker, looking down the vista of time, saw "rise in beauty the ideal home, state, nation, world."

Webster said: "The first principles of our Government are the truths of Divine Revelation."

Novalis holds that "The Christian religion is the root of all democracy, and the highest fact in the rights of man."

Goldwin Smith says: "The progress of nations and individuals follows in exact proportion in which they approach the gospel morality;" and that it was "from no other source than Christian Revelation that was derived that spirit * * which * * sent forth, on a crusade for the freedom and happiness of man, the best soldiers of the revolutionary armies of France — those of whom Hoche and Marceau were the gentle, brave, and chivalrous types."

Even Rousseau tells us, "The majesty of the Scriptures astonishes; their sanctity enraptures. The writings," he says, "of the philosophers, with all their pomp and parade, are trivial when compared with the sacred volume." "Is it possible," he asks, "that a work as simple, and yet as sublime, should be the work of men? Is it the style of an enthusiast or a sectary, inflated with ambition? The maxims, how sublime! * * the discourses of the Great Teacher, how wise and profound!"

And now are not these testimonies sufficient, independent of intrinsic evidences, to lead us to accept the Inspired Writings as suitable for popular use in our schools? If the influence of the Bible is, as it is proven to be by individual experience and the civil and social history of advanced peoples, favorable to good morals, intellectual improvement, industrial activity, frugal habits, just laws; if its truths awaken in the soul the spirit of the humane, the love of the beautiful, the noble, the heroic, and the sublime — why object? Is this not the ideal type? Has any other system of religion or of morals developed a nobler manhood, awakened loftier hopes or holier ambitions; inspired diviner equities or sweeter charities? If so, when and to whom has it been given? We travel back through the generations, and find superiority with those only who have marched down the periods in the light of God's Revelation.

In plea of submission to the removal of the Bible from the public schools some affect to believe in the sufficiency of the home, the church, and the school of the sectarian, to give the nation its required moral sentiment. But in this a fatal error is committed; for the reason, the homes, the churches, and the schools toward which we can now turn with confidence, but feebly represent the grand aggregate of social, political, and numerical power—are but mere rivulets compared with the mighty flood that is sweeping on with the Republic into the future.

Gold, luxury, ecclesiasticism, and infidelity have so far impaired the moral and religious sense of the nation that the model home, church, and school is fast becoming local and exceptional; soon, seemingly, to be scattered only here and there, like the retirements of the recluse of the Middle Ages. But even though there did not exist this disparity of moral and numerical force, there is present a serious defect in the proposition to place our children under the instruction of the religious sectary and dogmatist, as all experience shows. It is an experiment that has even proved in the end disastrous to the purity of faith and of conscience; especially, whenever the love of power, or when wealth and luxury, as now, have secularized the Church. The tendencies of the reachings, then, are politically pernicious and subversive of popular independence.

Collyer, Schermerhorn, Swing, and Cardinal McCloskey, religious exponents of more than six millions of our people, would exclude the Bible from the public schools, and place its exposition in the hands of the clergy, because it is only here, they assume, that its truths can be rightfully interpreted.

To the student of history and of the human heart these distinguished public utterances, at this time of increasing ostentation and of declining republican simplicity and virtue, are significant and portentious, and should lead us to guard with jealous care against the civil encroachments of the Church. The arguments of these advocates of clerical influence and authority clearly indicate a desire for the restoration of the old *regime* of absolutism, at least in matters of faith and of conscience. Freedom of individual will and thought in spiritual affairs is still an interdicted privilege with the ecclesiastic.

The Christian citizen, however, notwithstanding clerical authority, needs, neither for himself nor his child, the aid of any interpreter to comprehend the essential truths of the Bible. These are given us in the plain text of the Decalogue, the Beatitudes, the Universal Prayer, the Atonement, and the Resurrection, in language more explicit and effective than they can be through the mediumship of the school, man, or any commentator. Like the rigid and self-reliant Puritan, from whose foot-prints sprang free laws spontaneously, as flowers beneath tropic suns, we need no teacher but the Divine Spirit, no Confessor but the Father, no liturgy but the Bible. The true Church can, in spirit, exist without preacher, prelate, or Pope; and it is of such only, in fact, that the true Republic rises and augments in grandeur and power.

And the liberalist, as well as the strict constructionist, who affects to believe that our organic laws, Federal and State, prohibit Bible reading in the schools on the ground of sectarian influence, also falls into error; for the reason that, while it is true the people have, in their fundamental laws, provided against religious tests in official qualifications and the legislative establishing of religious organizations, they, at the same time, expressly recognize in their Bills of Rights or Constitutions the cardinal truths of Divine Revelation as the moral foundation of government. While they have wisely and jealously guarded against the encroachments of the Church or of sectarianism upon the rights of conscience and of the ballot, they have in most of the States, especially in the "Old Thirteen," plainly recognized in their organic Acts, as the standard of faith and ethics, the Christian and Hebrew Scriptures. It was not against the reading of the Bible in the schools that the fathers made constitutional provisions, but against the encroachments of ecclesiasticism, that undying vampire of liberty

—that power which had so long enthralled the intellect and the conscience of the race.

The evidence of this rests in the fact that, during the whole of the colonial period and the first half-century of the national, the use of the Bible in the public schools was felt to be a necessary feature of popular education; so much so as to assume the character and force of common law. Some of the colonies even legislated it into the schools; and the Congress of 1777, as well as that of 1781, on account of its "universal and great importance," as expressed by one Congressional Committee, did not deem it unworthy of their official attention and support.

From the moment that the spirit of American liberty began to stir in the hearts of a "poor people" in the north of England—from the hour it covertly fled from ecclesiastical and civil persecution across the heaths of Lincolnshire, down the Humber and out upon the North Sea—to the time when it had grandly embodied itself upon a new continent in the statutes of a great and free people, the Bible was its standard of faith; its supreme authority of moral appeal; its inspiration of law. And to-day, in letter and in spirit, running through bills of rights, preambles, constitutions, judicial oaths, and executive proclamations, it forms the religious and ethical standard of the nation—a standard which, not only the native-born, but the alien, be he Christian or Pagan, Jew or Mohammedan, is peculiarly bound by the most sacred obligations, as a recipient of the benefits of asylum, of the privileges of free citizenship, of the rights of manhood, to accept, formally at least, with respectful consideration and grateful deference.

It is accepted by the political philosopher as axiomatic that without popular morality there can be no substantial popular government; and as it is also an established truth that, without a recognition of God and His moral government as revealed in the Scriptures, there can be no sound morality, it logically follows, that Scriptural readings in our schools are not only constitutionally consistent, but strictly legal. It is the plea only of the sophist, who brings the charge of sectarianism against the reading of the Bible in the American public schools; for it is plainly written in legislative Act, and in national custom, that its philosophy forms the moral woof and warp of our political faith and our entire organic law — that in spirit, Christianity, by constitutional and conventional recognition, is the established faith of the State; and that the Bible, as the text-book of that faith, is the standard of national ethics. Therefore, critically considered, it is the Atheist, the Jesuit, the rigid ecclesiastic—hereditary enemies of a popular Bible and of popular government, who are the sectarians in fact, and against whom their own charge strictly rests.

To declare the simple reading of the Bible in the schools, or the chanting there of the Psalms, or the Lord's Prayer—that sublime " Litany of nations "—sectarian, is the acme of absurdity, is the subterfuge of a narrow and jealous dogmatism, and can only be pronounced by him whose heart has never yet glowed in the full light of either written or unwritten revelation, nor truly thrilled beneath the touch of their spiritual forces.

And yet we hear those in our midst assuming to have been called of God to expound, defend, and to scatter among men the truths of His Word, so darkened in comprehension, or so recreant to duty, as to willingly withhold it from the great needy masses by such construction of the letter and spirit of our organic laws as to render its use in our schools ostensibly a violation of civil and religious rights. In their professed and dramatic zeal for religious and political liberality they would not only remove from popular reach the very foundation of the faith they pretentiously teach, but in fact the moral foundation of the government itself. Out of a pretended sense of equity, and an assumed Christian deference to the prejudices of the Pagan, the Infidel, the Jewish, and the Red Republican—in their extreme catholic desire to bend and accommodate our institutions and our customs to the religious, social, and political views of their inconoclasts of liberty, they willingly subvert the meaning of the most plain and sacred provisions and influences of fundamental law. They anxiously make concessions in the name of liberty, but not to those who have established and maintained it; but rather to those who, in every period of their power, have trodden down with Gothic fierceness the prophets and Messiahs of freedom.

Instead of a wise and just tolerance in the exercise of republican liberty, these men seem drunken with an excess of the sentiment; or else but express a venal ambition for popularity, or for power and its forms, which sickens over the virtues and simplicities of republicanism. If republican, their inconsistency is only equaled by that of the statesman whose rhetorical fastidiousness led to more concern for the cadence of a period than for the fall of a commonwealth."

As additional evidence of clerical drift, we here call attention to a virtual indorsement of Collyer,

Schermerhorn, Swing, and McClosky, from a source which we might least expect. At the last anniversary of the "Conference Educational Society of the Methodist Episcopal Church North," of California, its Vice-President gave official utterance to the following language: He says: "It is my candid opinion that our public schools must eventually be Bibleless and prayerless. So long as all do not believe in Christ and the Scriptures, I do not see how we can stand by our principles as Americans, and yet force people to hear the Bible read as the Word of God. In the interests of Christianity, I advise that Bible reading * * * * be discontinued in the public schools, when persistent objection is made * * * * by lawful patrons."

Such is the language of L. L. Rogers, Vice-President of the "Conference Educational Society of the Methodist Episcopal Church North," of California— an expression of sentiment remarkable for two reasons: First, because it is tacitly an official declaration of a loss of faith, by a prominent body of Protestant clergymen, in the progressive energies of Christianity. Second, because it is an unequivocal acknowledgment of hopeless defeat in the maintaining of a traditional feature of the American system of public instruction —an unconditional surrendering to the enemy of one of the great moral guaranties of our government.

To analyze the opinion of this clerical representative, and weigh it by the old, the heroic standard of American faith, as well as by the orthodox standard of true Methodism, we are more convinced than ever that Christianity with us is losing its heroism; is becoming formalized, and that Gladstone was correct when he lately said: "The marked want of the Church to-day is the want of great men as leaders "—men, we will add, who have a supreme faith in God, in His Word, and in His providence — men who have the nerve and the fidelity to 'stand by principle,' though "all do not believe in Christ and the Scriptures "— men who, discerning the indissoluble relations between the Bible and free government, are ready to labor, at any cost, to interweave its ethics and its republican sentiments into the primary education of the masses.

Ordained expositors of the Bible may recommend its exclusion from the public schools, and thereby practically contradict their assumption of faith in its divinity, its philosophy, and its prepotent influences; but they may as well arouse themselves first as last to the overshadowing fact that a crisis is approaching upon this question, in which they must either advance and take a more consistent stand, or retreat and make a more consistent profession. The prophecy of "coming revolution" is no idle dream. He who can not hear its onward tread is deaf to the footsteps of the future.

The re-establishing of the early custom of reading the Bible in the schools, and the rescue of our system of public instruction from anti-republican influences, is to be a leading question of the near future; destined to force to the front, unmasked, every element of our national life, and lead to a more satisfactory solution of the American idea of government and of governmental auxiliaries.

The Bible in the schools is a question we cannot evade if we would. It involves principles which are essential and vital to liberty; and, as a result, it is now reassuming its early national importance — is again irresistibly crowding itself, as if by divine necessity, upon our serious attention. No escape from finally meeting it can be made, either behind the subterfuge of "independent schools," as recommended by the sectarian or the timid, or through the specious plea of illiberalism, as assumed by the infidel or the secularist. The limit is being approached, beyond which "compromise" becomes an empty term, and timidity, indifference, or infidelity virtually become political treason.

To relinquish our hold to any essential extent upon the public school, and substitute for it the "independent," would ultimately be fatal, inasmuch as it not only involves finally a division of the school funds, but would increase and intensify sectarian prejudice, sectionalize the national sympathies and aims, and thereby weaken the bonds of public unity.

Our common schools, with common support, with common text-books, and with a common faith, would become, finally, bonds of union, strong and binding even as is the Constitution.

It becomes us to meet this question boldly, and with no offers of compromise—determined to maintain inviolate the original idea and faith of the fathers in the management of our common schools. It seems incomprehensible that men who, by their habits of thought and professions of faith, ought to understand the political as well as moral influences of the Bible—in fact, its utter indispensability to popular government—should be found willingly withholding from the public school this guaranty of civil and religious freedom. But such are the incongruities of the times. We, however, rest in the faith that every great emergency involving sacred public interests calls up, at the right hour, its hero or its heroes, to inspire and to lead. So, in the coming conflict of Bible or no Bible in the public schools, of national loyalty to the Revealed Law of God, or national apostasy, we are sure that, in the fullness of time, regardless of secular or ecclesiastical opinion or decree, the spirit embodied will come, which shall lead the Republic to a higher and a grander life. Melancholy as is the reflection, it is nevertheless true that it is mainly through the defective judgment, apathy, or apostasy of the representatives of religious sentiment that our youth are now going forth to assume the sacred trusts of citizenship with no higher inspiration, beyond the uncertain moral influences of secular education, than that of the cold legalism of the materialist; the narrow dogmas of the ecclesiastic; the sensuous tenets of the spiritist; the lawless creed of the communist—antagonistic forces, in which are inherent and expanding the elements of irrepressible conflicts—conflicts in which all the tragedies of history will finally be repeated and intensified—wherein will finally be fulfilled the vision, in which John saw the angel with thrusting sickle, and the great wine-press with its sea of blood flowing even to the "horse-bridles" of the armies of God. This is as clearly defined to the vision of philosophy as were the tragedies of the irrepressible conflict between freedom and slavery to the prescient eyes of Seward and his coadjutors. Let the fool only believe that republics may flourish without God; that God does not manifest Himself in history, rewarding the nations that walk in His law, and punishing those that depart from it.

True, the hour is resonant with the voices of a mighty skepticism, regal in power of research, of analysis and of deduction; proclaiming " No God but nature;" no revelation but her silent mountains, her wide-spread plains, her heaving seas, her glowing suns; and declaring man, the offspring only of her pulseless womb—his spiritual, moral, and social evolution the result simply of a blind, self-acting, inevitable law. But all this dies in echo as we stand by the mighty Angel of History, and see him write on every page of the nation's annals, "Lo! God is here; though ye see Him not, yet, behold the light of His presence, the foot-prints of His passing, the desolations of His vengeance."

And now, in conclusion, I will add: if we would protect the integrity of our institutions; if we would preserve liberty to ourselves and transmit it to others, we must be loyal to the Bible—that great obstacle to the advance of ecclesiastical and civil despotism—that great instrument of freedom which lies beneath all our Bills of Rights, Constitutions, and laws, and from which our entire civil polity draws its inspiration and power. We should cherish it as sacredly as we cherish liberty itself; for, without it, the voice of experience and of philosophy tell us there can be no liberty, no protection for the weak, no guarantee of private or public rights.

Said De Bow, in embodying the civilization of a country in its aristocracy: "The masses are molded into soldiers and artisans by intellect, just as matter and the elements of nature are made into telegraphs and steam-engines. If you educate the poor, they soon forget all that is necessary in the common transactions of life. To make an aristocrat in the future," he says, "we must sacrifice a thousand paupers. Yet we would, by all means, make them—make them permanent too, by laws of entail and primogeniture."

This, oh! ye brown-visaged, rough-handed, brawny

armed son of toil—patient builder of the world's material and moral grandeurs—is the social and political theory of the De Bows—those who would rear, as did the Spartan, their civic and social pillars upon the quivering heart of Labor. But how quickly does this cold, imperious, and barbaric figure shiver, from vital transitions; and then blush, with warmer blood; and now glow, with sublime inspirations of equity, when placed in the light of the Inspired Word — when brought beneath the focus of this great Beam of effulgent essence from the heart of the Infinite. The friends of civilization, and of civil and religious freedom in all lands, should venerate it; for what instrument or agent has accomplished so much for the aggrandizement of man? Through the influence of that single Bible which Luther found at Erfurt there has been written a grander and more imperishable civil and social history than that of all the preceding ages. The impulses of that very Volume are to-day throbbing and chafing in the world's great channels of sympathy, of thought, of language, and of law. It pulsates in the heart of the steamship, in the furnace of the factory, along the electric currents of the telegraph, in the types of the printing-press, in the shafts and galleries of the mine, in the battle-hymns of our poets, in the prophecies of our seers, and in the orations of our statesmen. It flashed upon the steel of our soldiery along the Potomac, the James, and the Rio Grande. It struck the fetters from the limbs of our slaves, and is now giving light, faith, and conscience to the heart of the master. The Bible is the great hope of the free as well as of the oppressed in all lands, and will be in all periods of the future, until the fullness of time is complete, and the great dial-finger of the ages shall cease its revolutions forever and forever.

www.ingramcontent.com/pod-product-compliance
Lightning Source LLC
Chambersburg PA
CBHW020252090426
42735CB00010B/1891